ISBN: 9781500510879

Cover: "Breeze" by Cassandra Gordon-Harris
Rincon Studios
Roswell, NM 88201
https://casgohart.wixsite.com/c-gordon-harris

For Charlie

Just a Little Magic

to begin.......

These graphite drawings were created during the 2020 Covid 19 pandemic. A fellow artist suggested I put them in a book with poetry. On my bookshelf was a spiral bound file of poems by my friend Sandra J Melcher, who, before she died, gave me that file saying, "Perhaps you can do something with these." They were long, epic, deep soul-searching prose that touched my heart. That was nearly 20 years ago. I have take short passages from Sandra's' thought- provoking poems and put them together with my light and whimsical drawings to create a joyful and magical journey of the soul of two artists.

"I felt the powerful wing beats of bird guides and the padding feet of animal spirits,
Above and around us, but did not know how to reach out to them."

From "Lost & Godness" ©1993

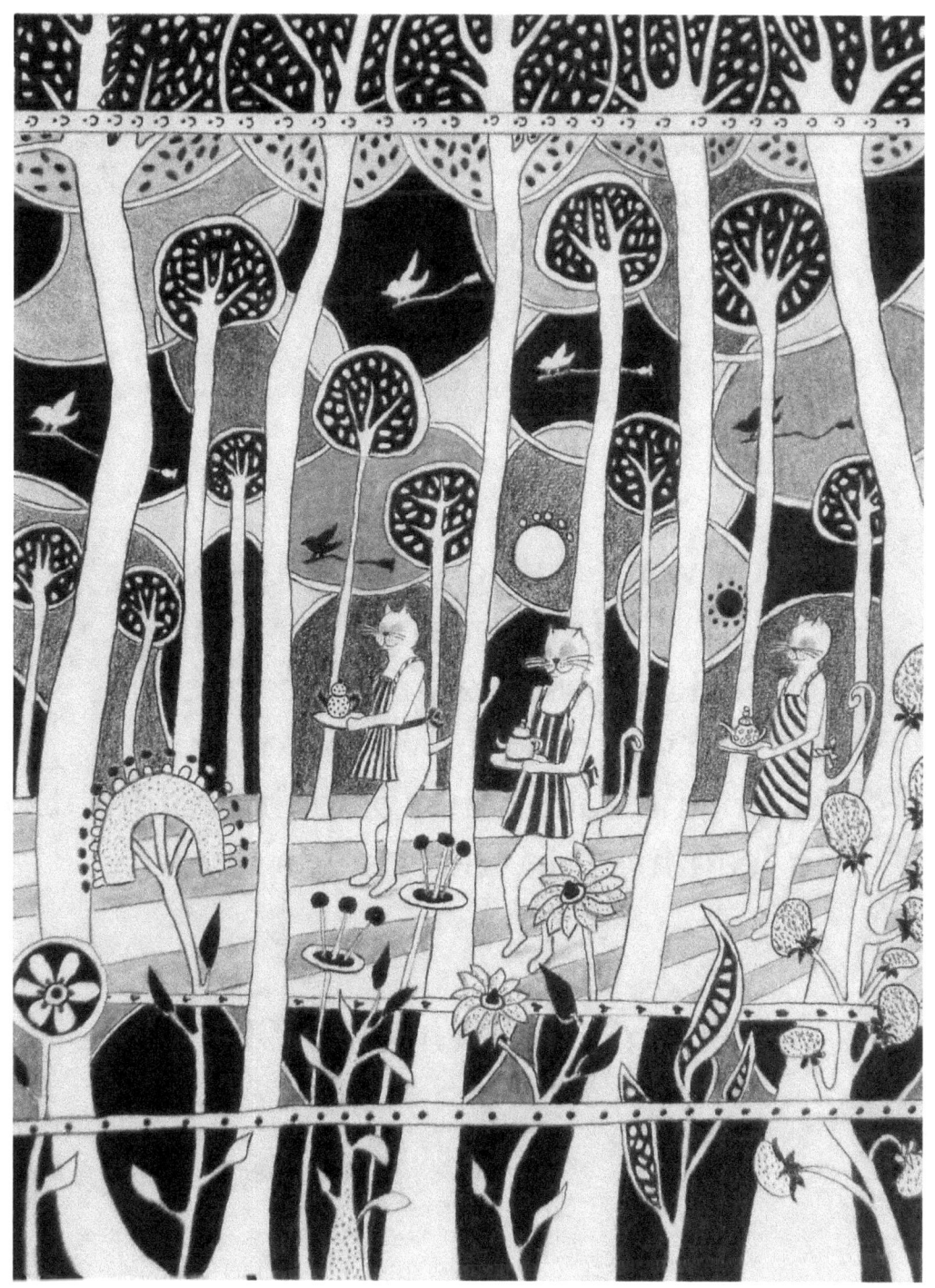

Tea

"You walk my soul and I become
pure energy,
Able to cross over mind barriers,
Seeing with a clear vision of truth.
Experiencing each other as points of light.
You lead me into fresh fields of glory."

From "Soul Walk", ©1997

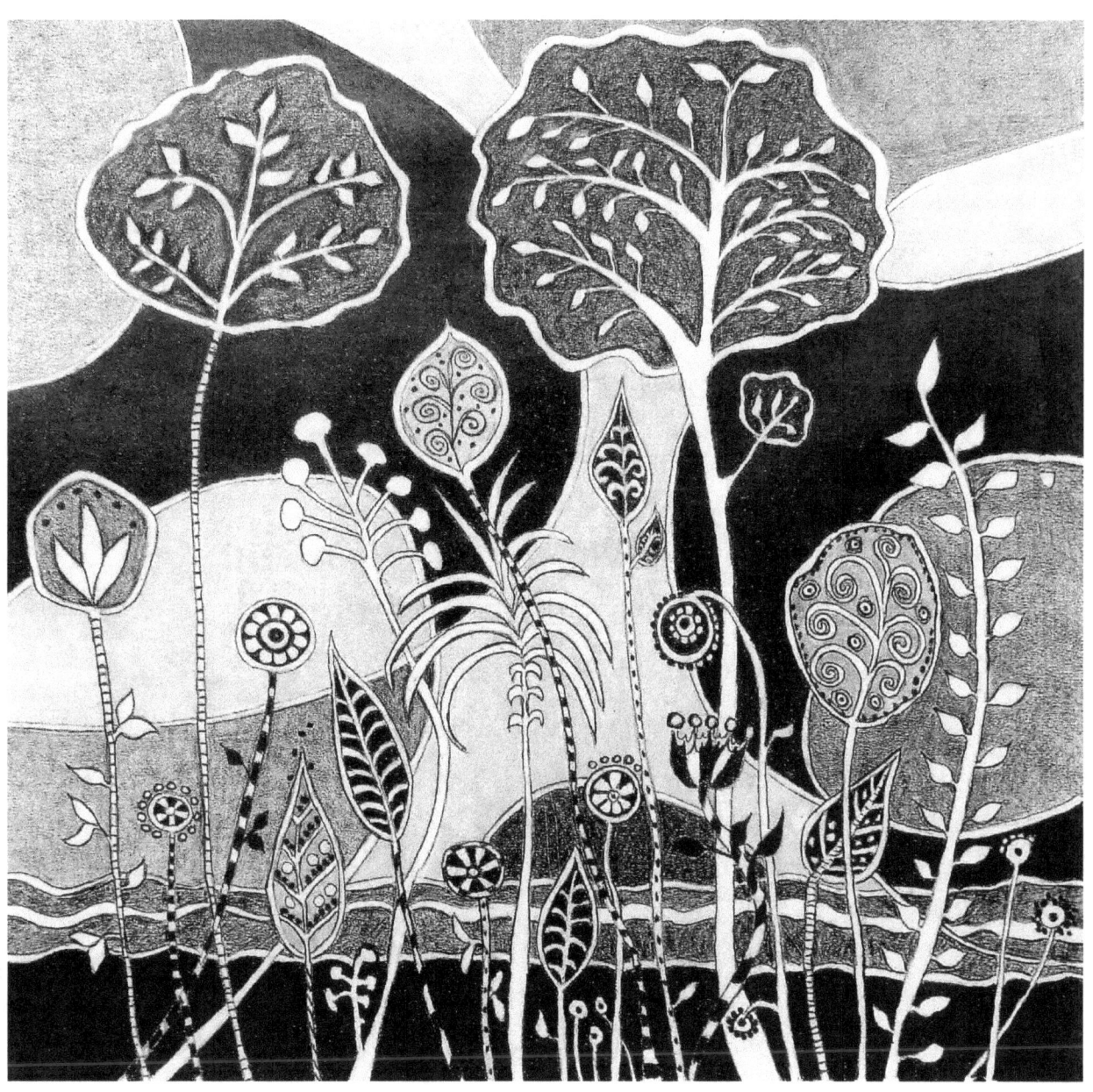

Plants

"She moves through progressively
higher levels of consciousness
with ease,
Gathering knowledge multi-dimensionally
through exponentially
expanded senses.
She is ourselves and our sentient
Earth, birthing into undreamed
realms and realities.
She is Starchild
loosed into vibrational frequencies and the endless light."

From "Starchild" ©1999

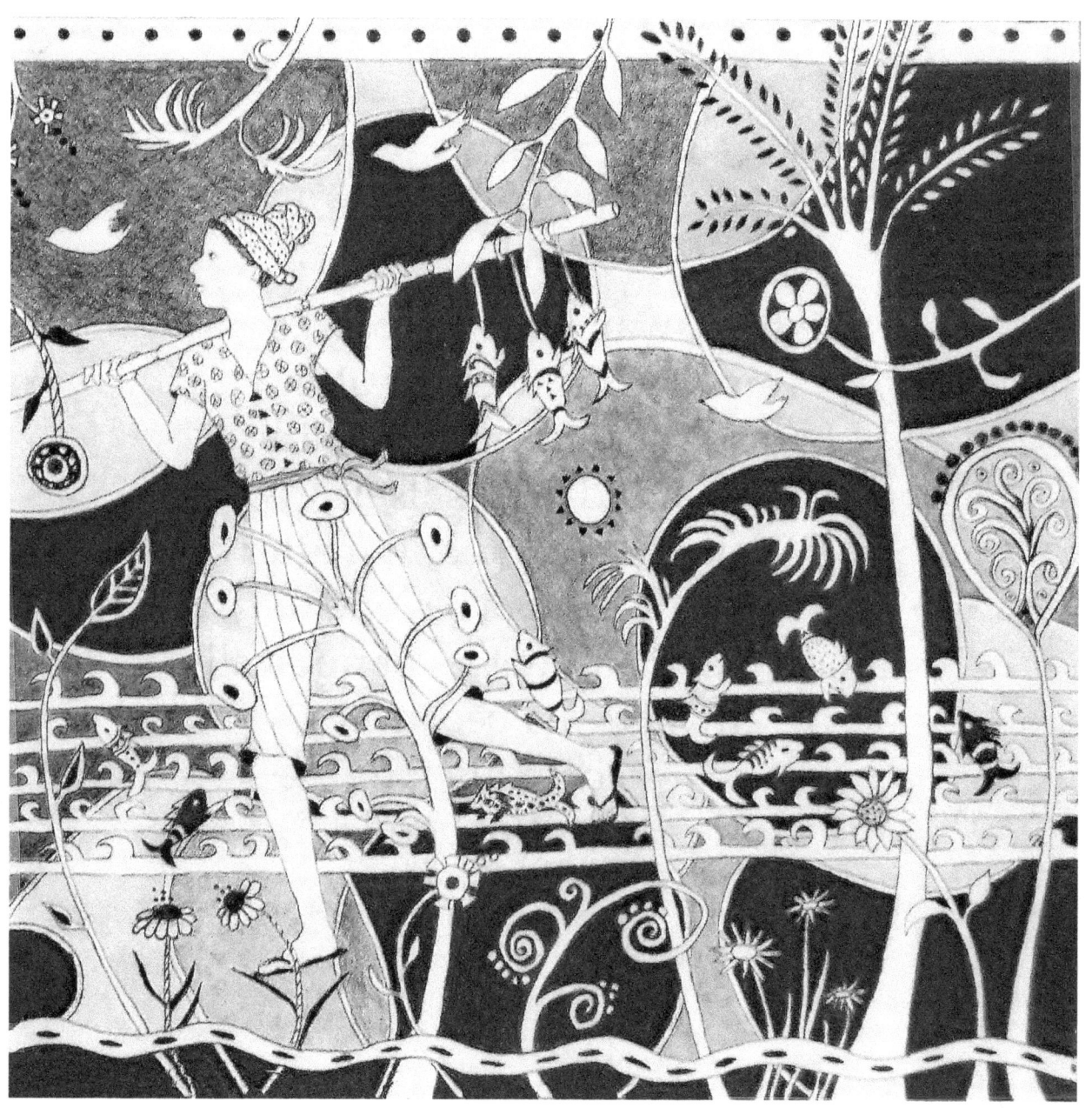

Fish

"I tear away layers of masks
my hidden face retreats
I grasp the illusions of reality
my mind erases itself
My body is anchored in matter
my spirit soars beyond
I am set new parameters periodically
my persona becomes
rebellious
Free of mortal bonds
I am pure energy
and my path is clear."

From "Spiritual Bloodhound", ©1986

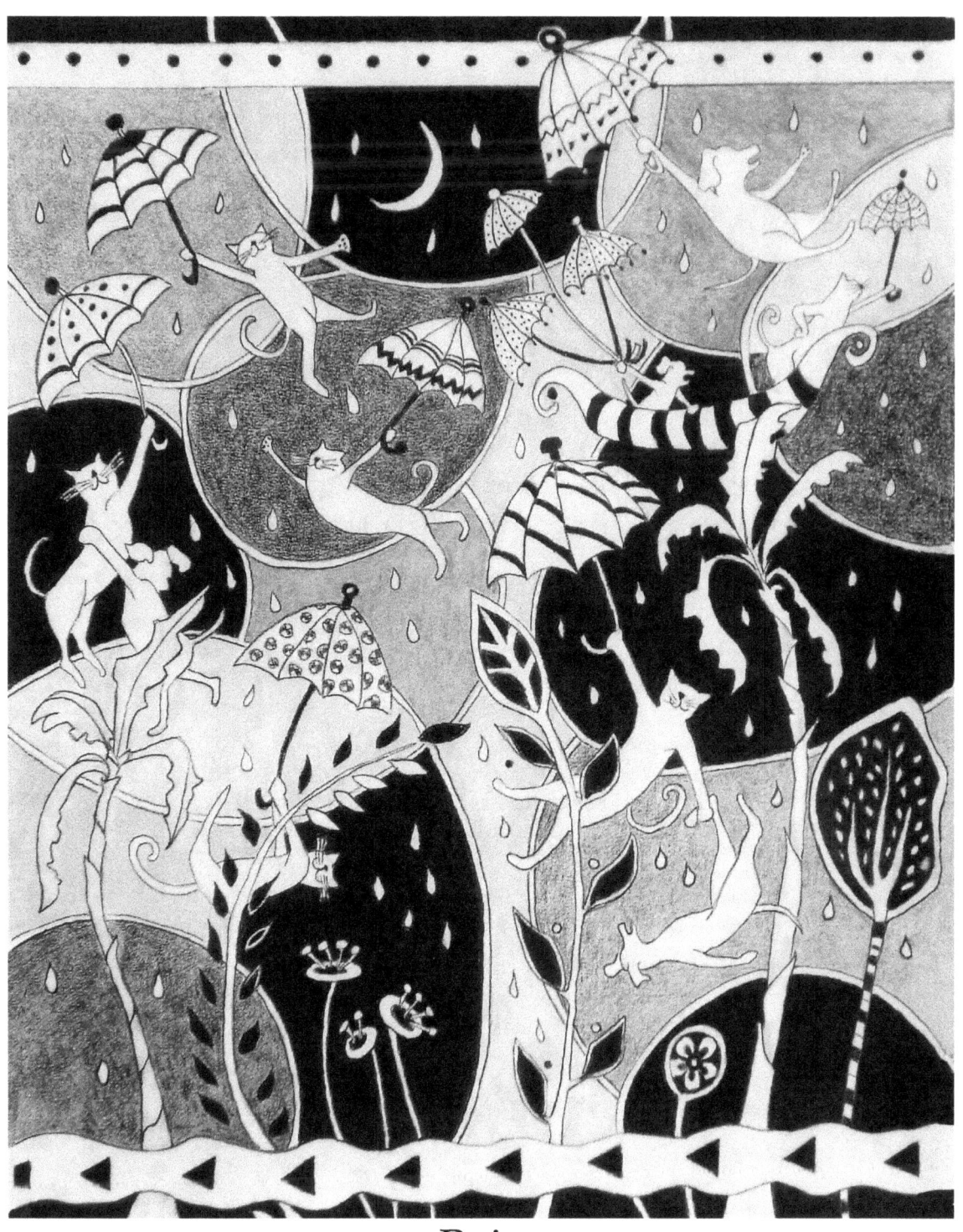

Rain

"You are like the the birds of the air
flying and diving through the adventures
and lessons of life."

From "Find the Child Within", ©2002

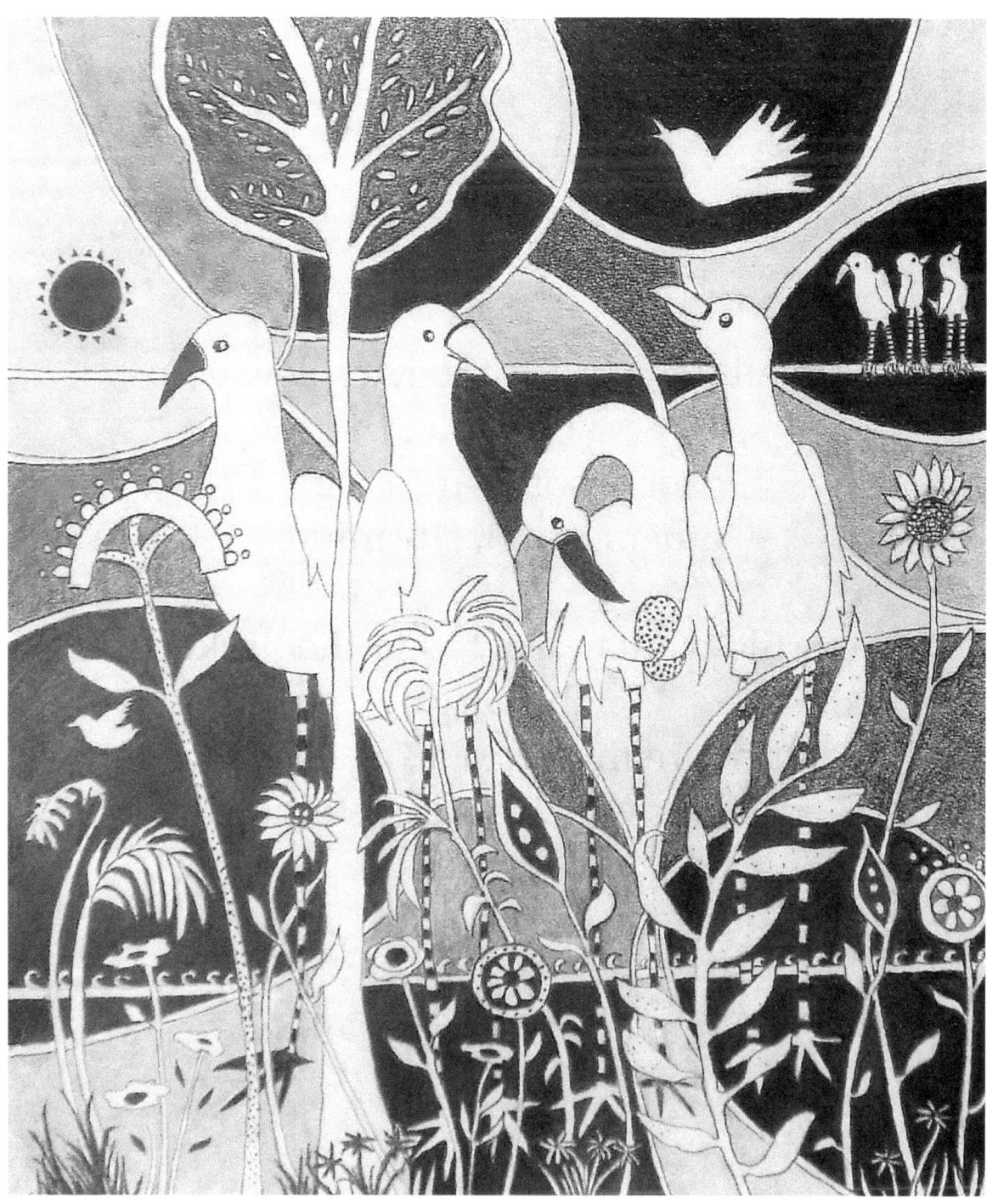

Birds

"I am all the winds that ever blew across
your soul,
some soft, caressing,
others harsh, storming.

I am fertile woman, rooted to the darkness of
the earth
in which are mysterious, ageless secrets
out of which spring eternal
new life."

From "Who Am I", ©1988

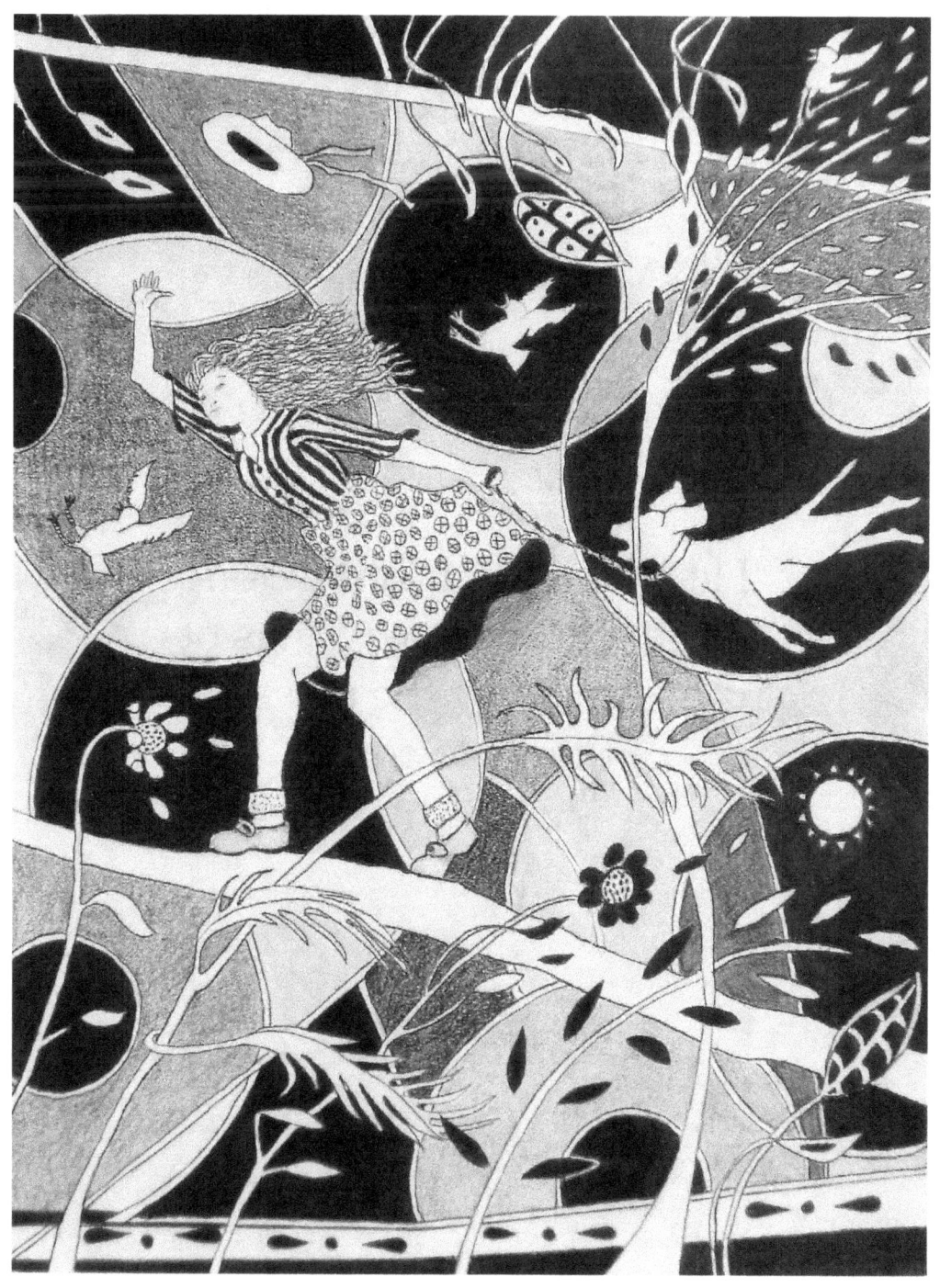

Wind

"I leaped and played among
the galaxies put on wings of
future and saw the message
of things to come."

From "Cosmic Venus" ©1978

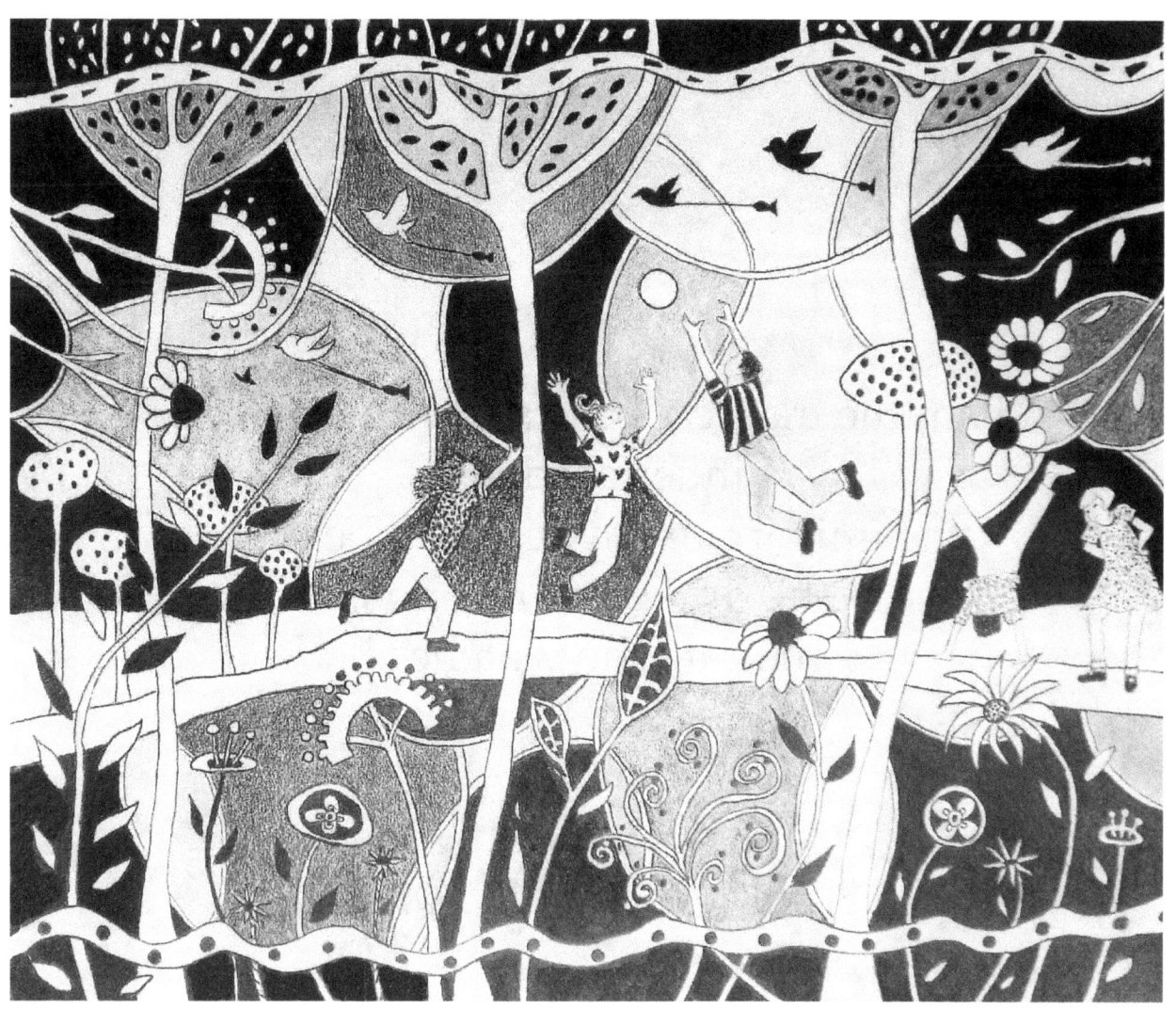

Play

"I am the magical beasts of your deepest,
inner gardens,
the unicorn of shyness and beauty,
the dragon of legends.
the cat who watches."

From "Who am I", ©1988

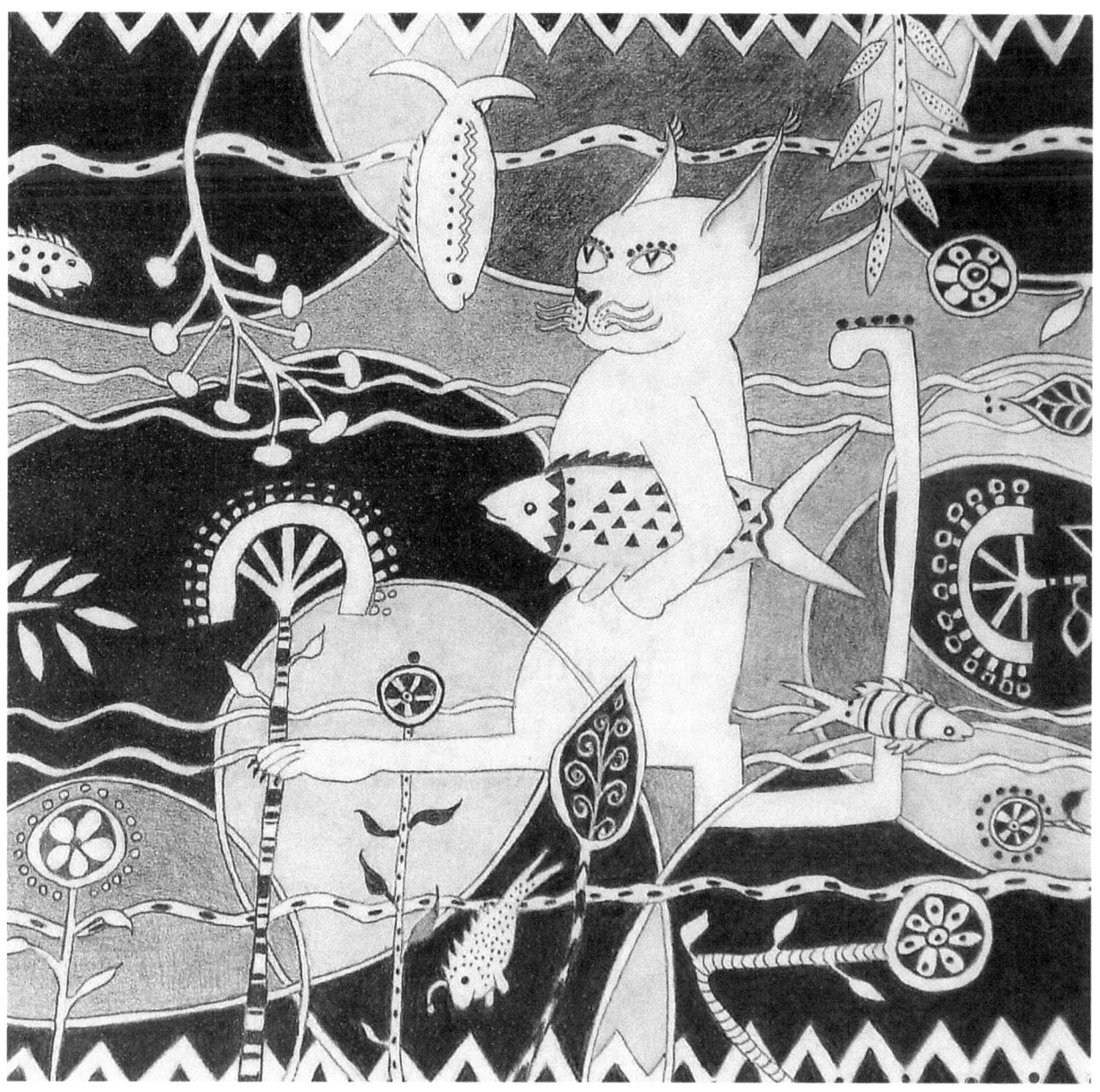

Catfish

"I soared among the stars
and heard the sound
of ages
rushing by."

From "Cosmic Venus", ©1978

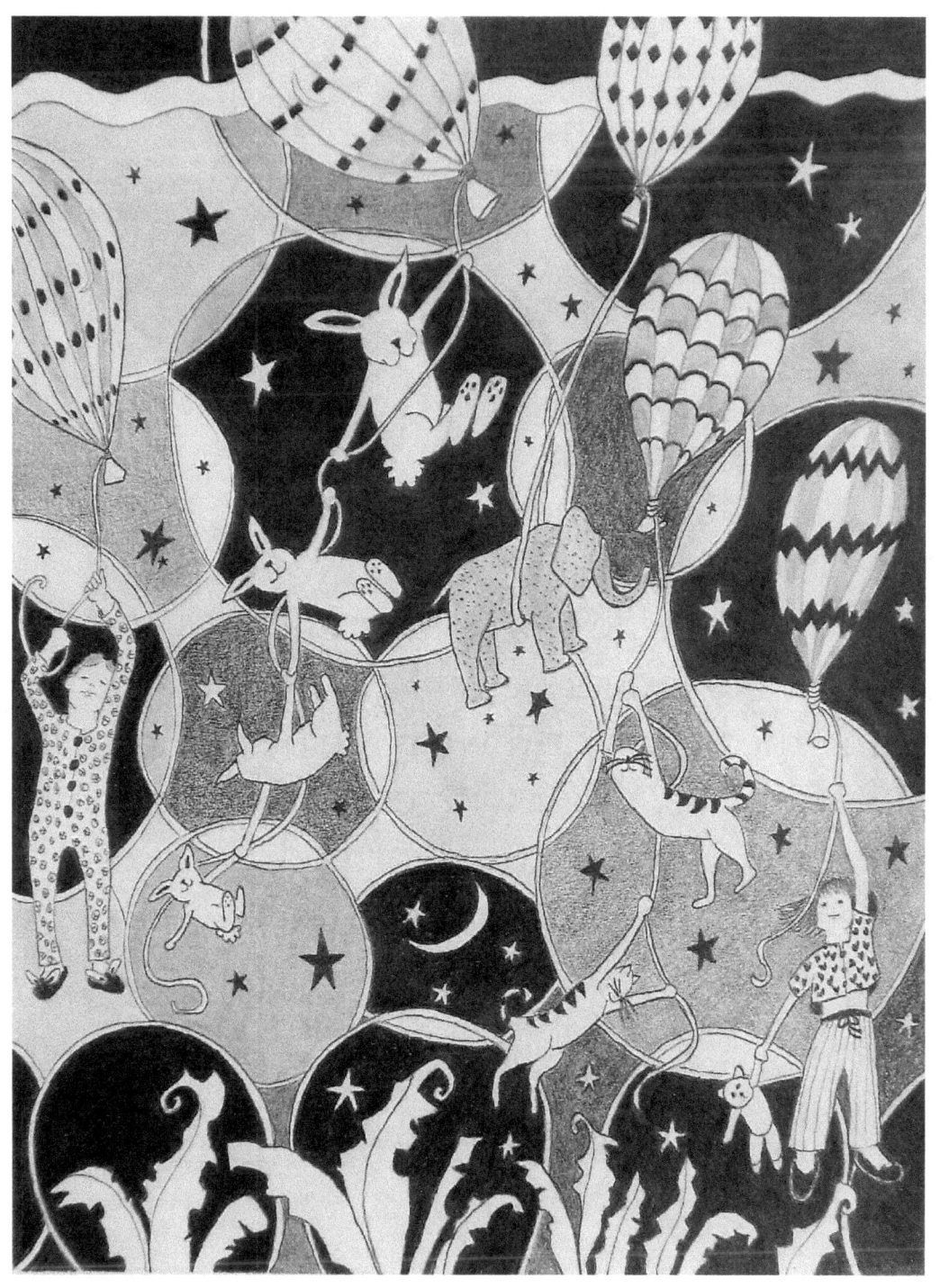

Balloons

"Like the butterfly we emerge, opening the
self to new perceptions,
stretching wings, sensing vast spaces
new levels of awareness,
No longer heavy and bound.
Tasting the new world we have been thrust into,
it is joyous, filled with endless horizons,
we are transformed,
translucent and free."

From "Butterflies and Transformation"
©1993

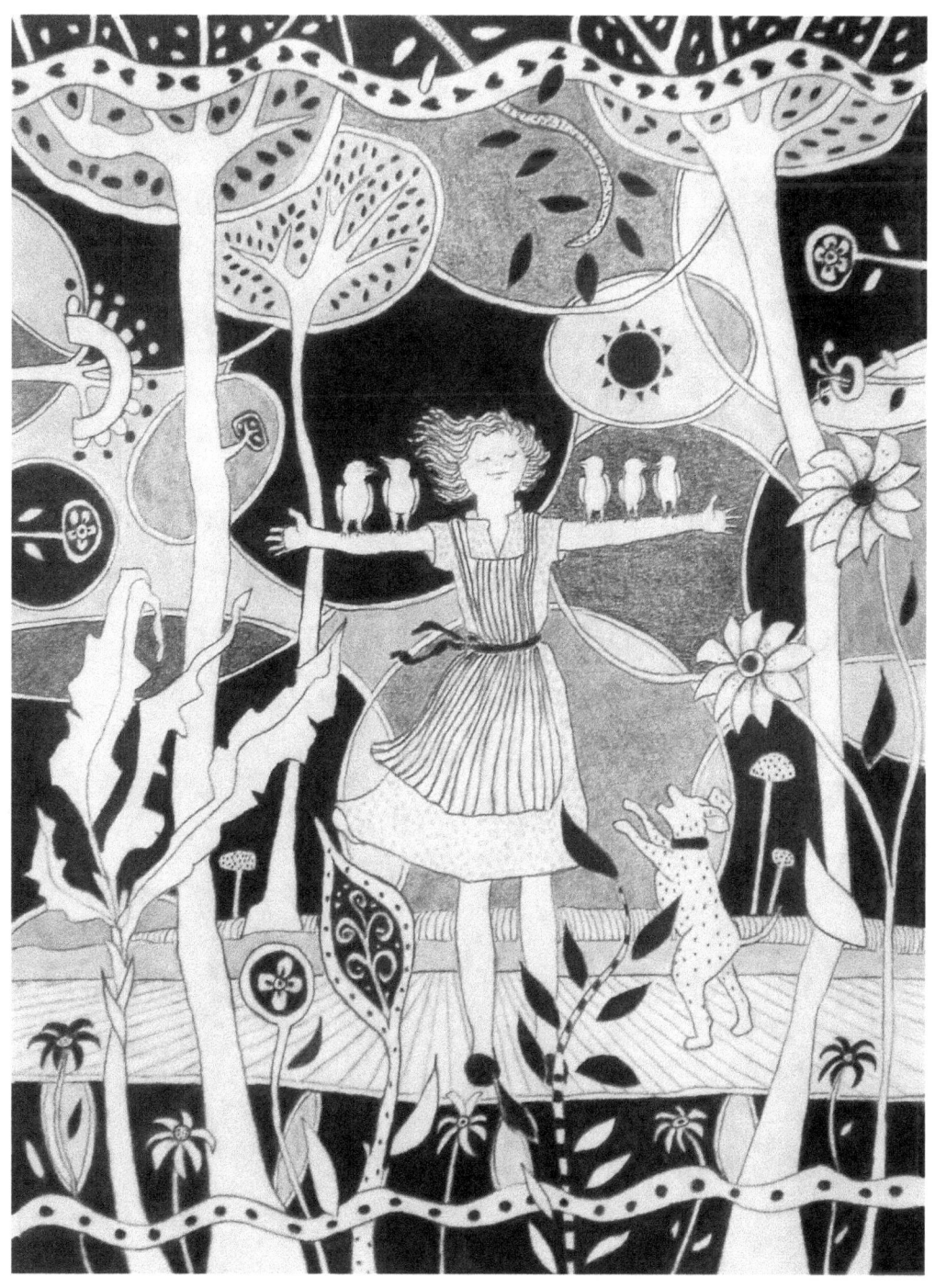

Breeze

"Flowers crowned, I flow in and out
of make-believe
and reality
I gaze out from inner image, tailoring outside
to inside
Innocent of experience, skimming over line,
laughing and hopeful."

From "Madonna of the Pillow", ©1988

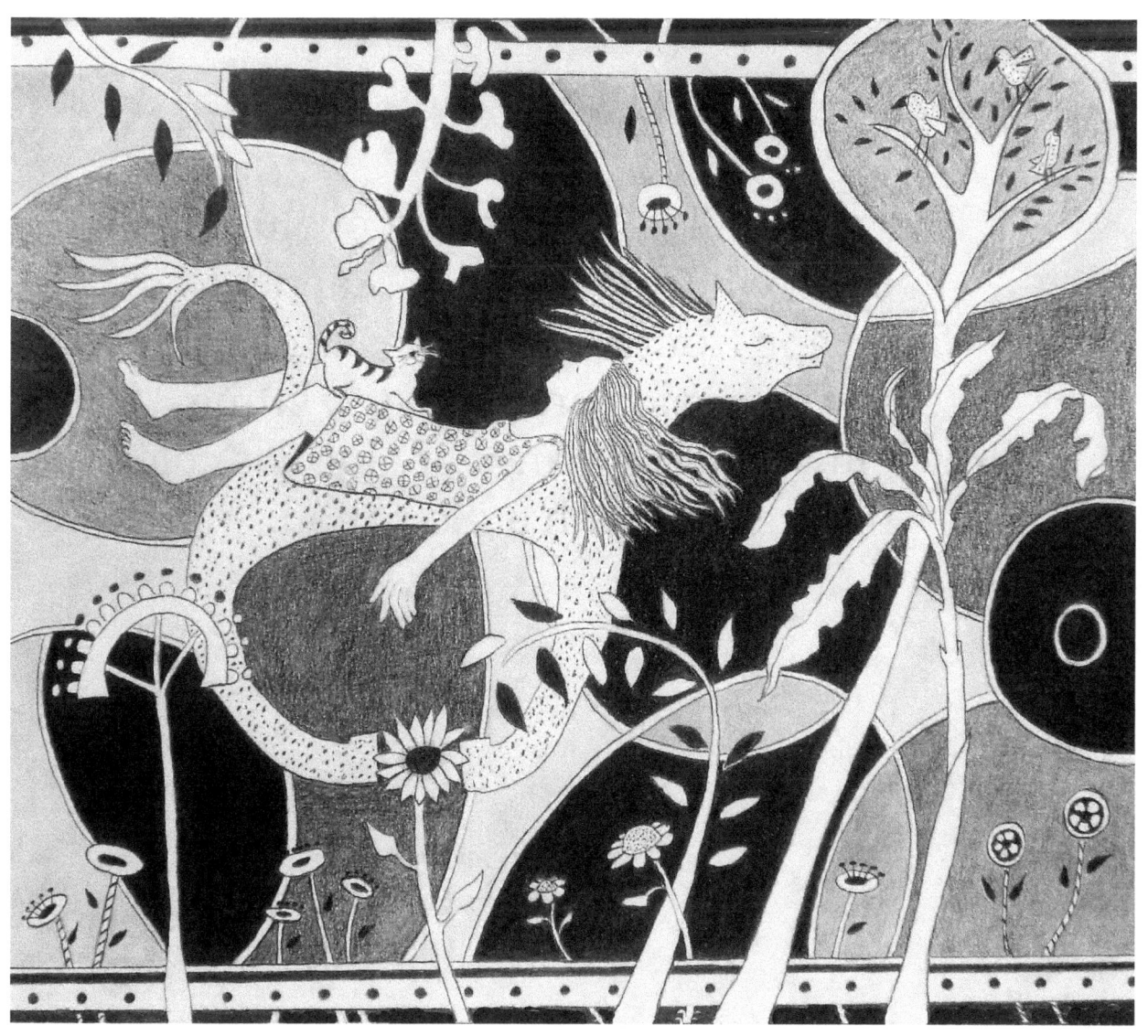

Rocking Horse

"The soul walk is the coming evolution
upon whose threshold I stand.
Emerging from a cocoon of slumber,
Veils of confusion and paradox lifting,
I stretch my butterfly wings of glorious color,
and tremble with anticipation."

From "Soul Walk" ©1997

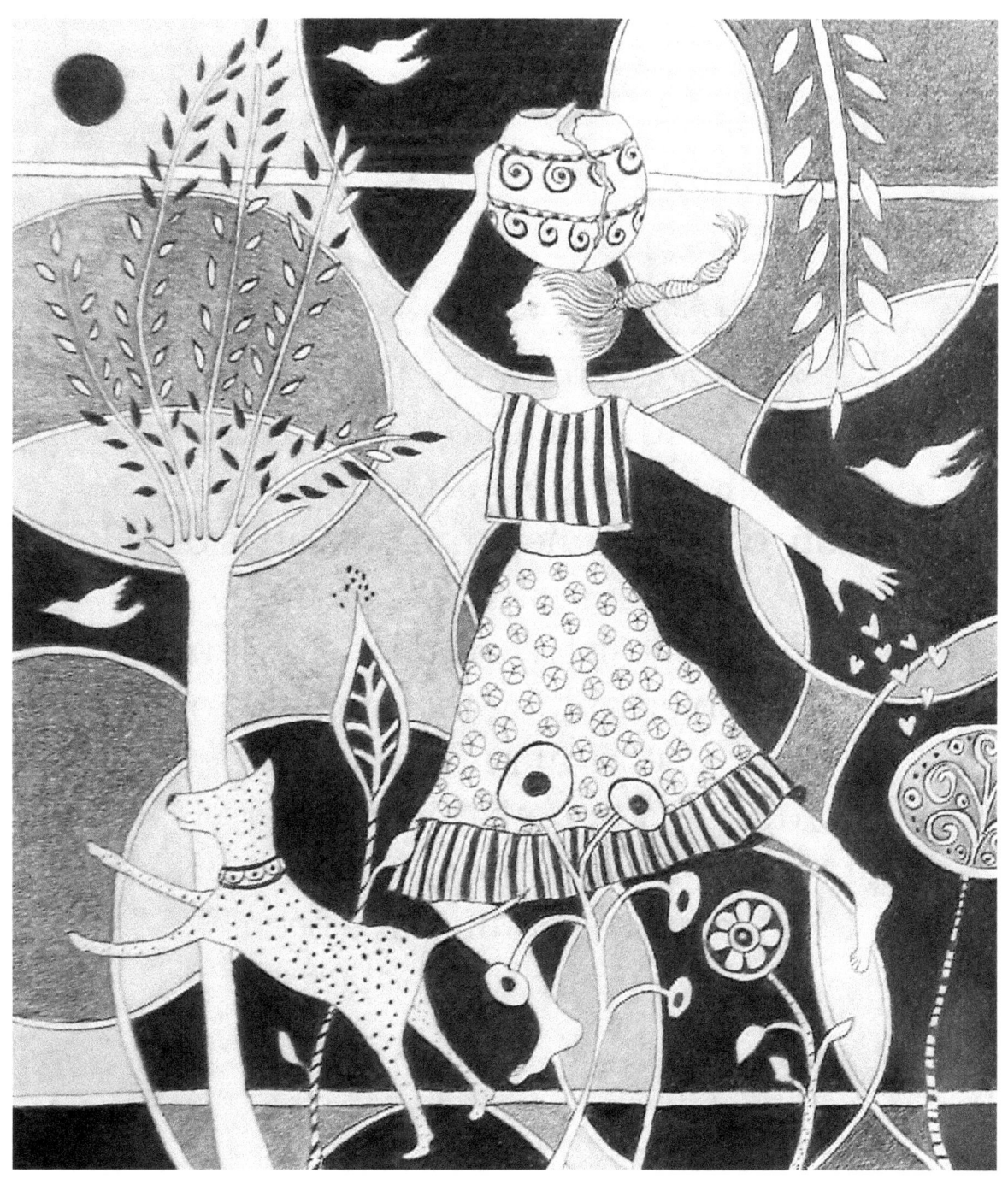

Joy

"We did not hear the collective Mother, keening
over her slaughtered children,
Instead we stepped back into the mirrors of illusion,
gathered more stuff around us,
saw 'you' only as 'other', the polarities of belief
systems,
brother against sister, nation against nation.
Squabbled among the carcasses of
historical re-creation,
destined to repeat their errors,
kept constantly examining our 'feet of clay',
when we should have been
looking up to the stars."

From "Lost and Godness", ©1993

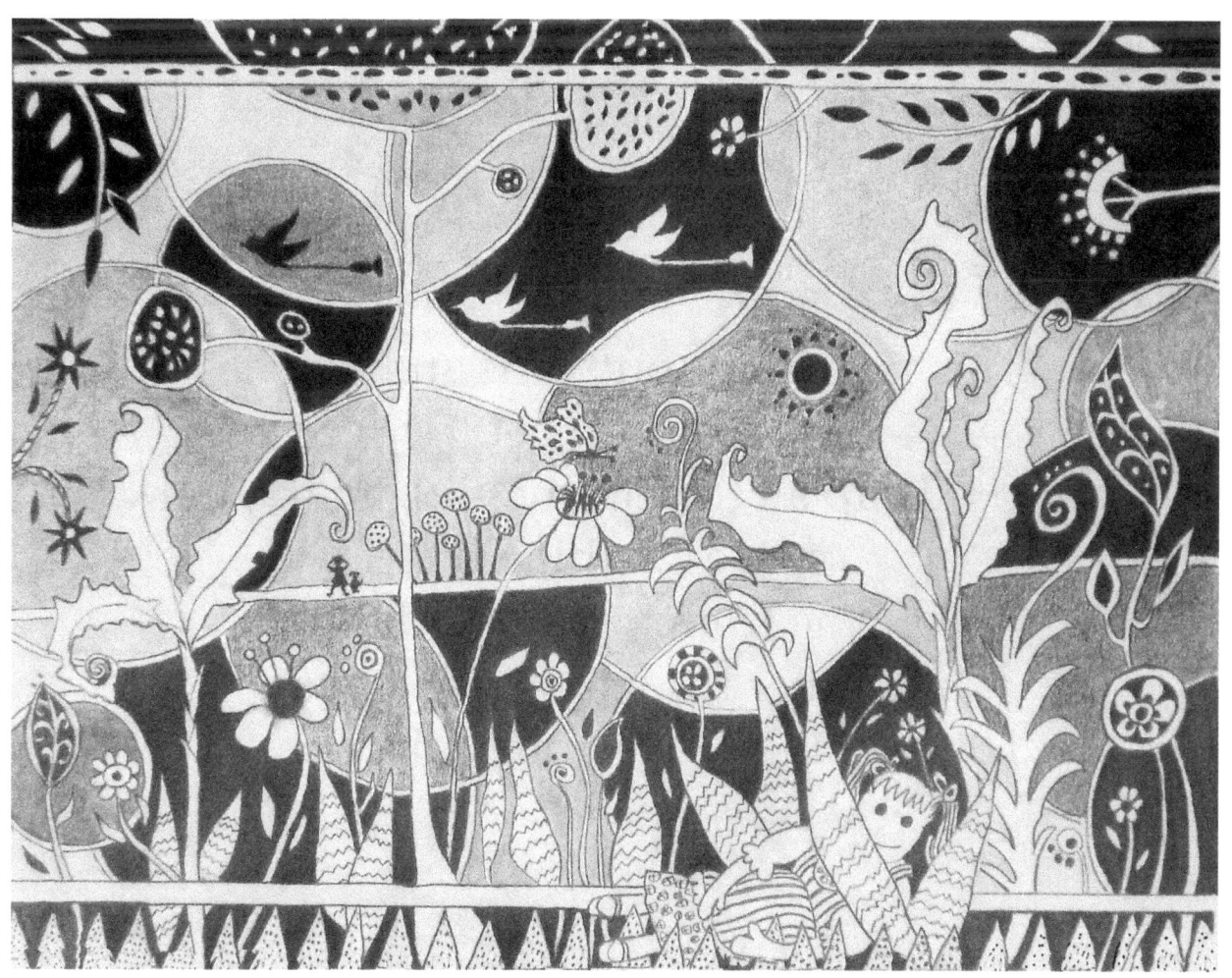

Lost Doll

"This love flows outward and touches
all you meet.
It also fills up all the empty, sad, angry, dark,
spaces within you.
Some from just yesterday,
and other from long, long ago.
Let my music take your pain away."

From "Find the Child Within" ©2002

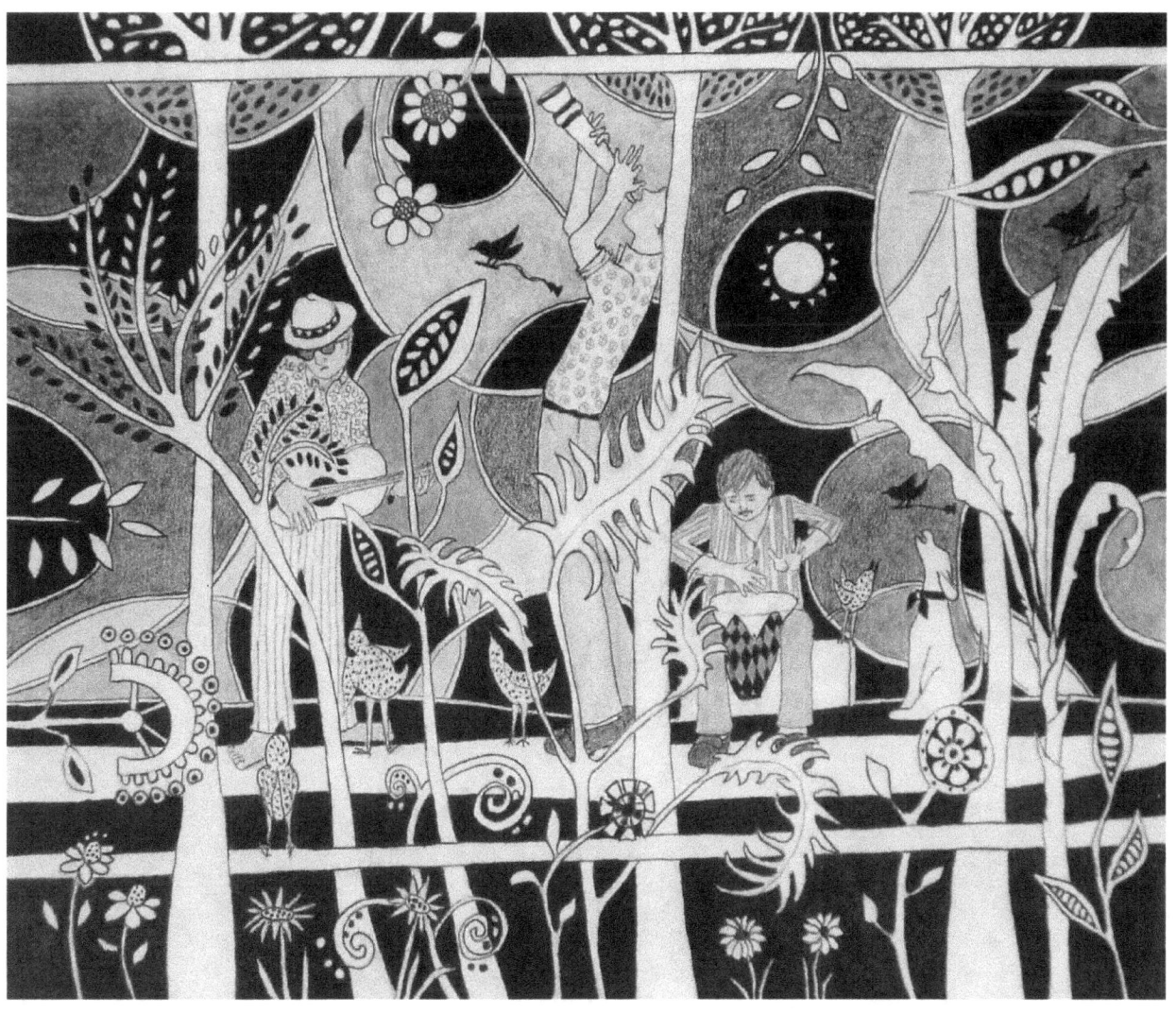

Music

"I look out upon this world
and I see growth,
yes I do.
I look out and see man stumble,
yes I do,
fall down hard.
I throw out a ray of love,
love and truth,
yes I do,
truth and light."

From "God's View", ©1997

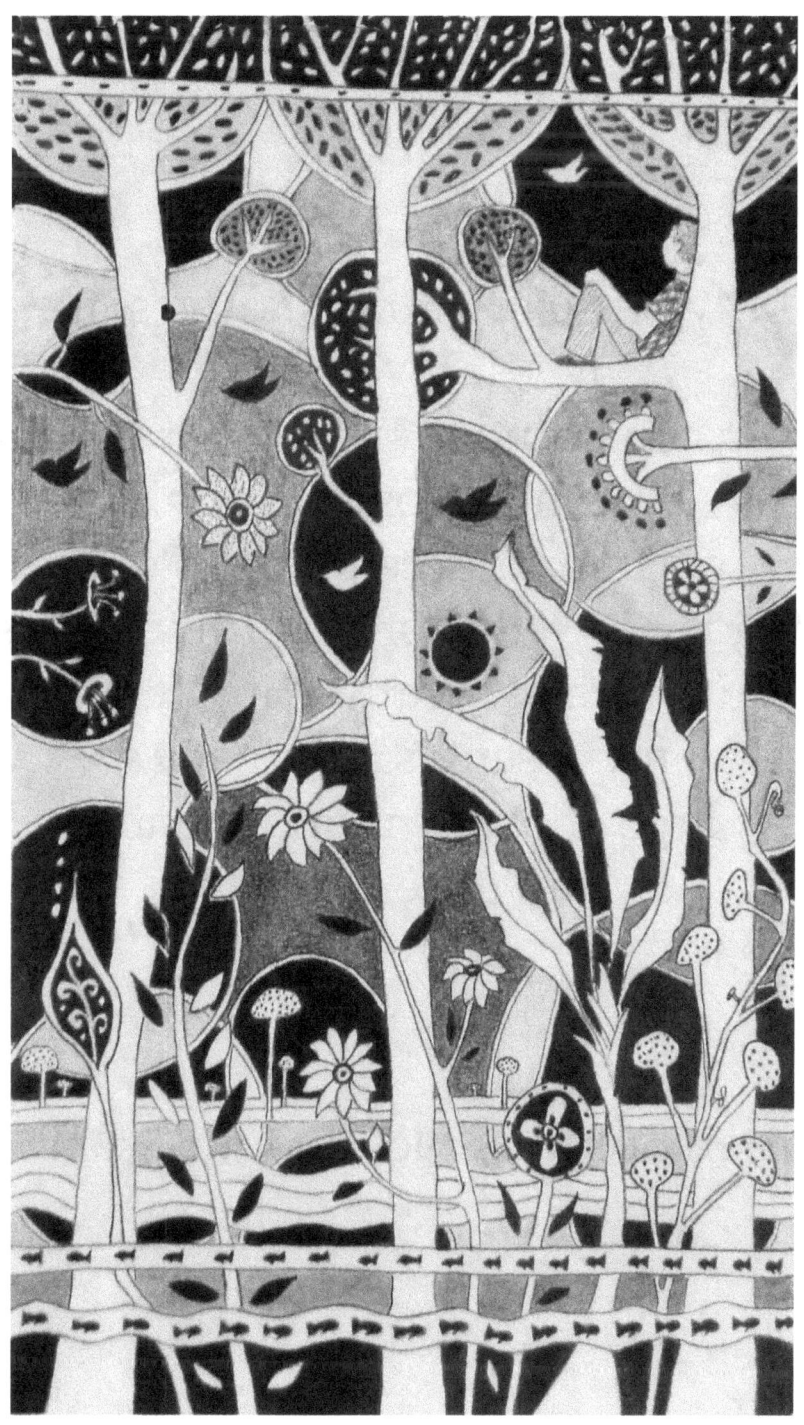

Canopy

"My sense of infinity is awesome
my self revels in joy
I am commanded from inner spaces
the microcosm within,
I become interference patterns of beauty.
Stand at the edge of new dimensions,
Am aware of breathtaking realities
my assent is automatic.
Free of heavy mortal bonds
I am pure energy."

From "Spiritual Bloodhound", ©1986

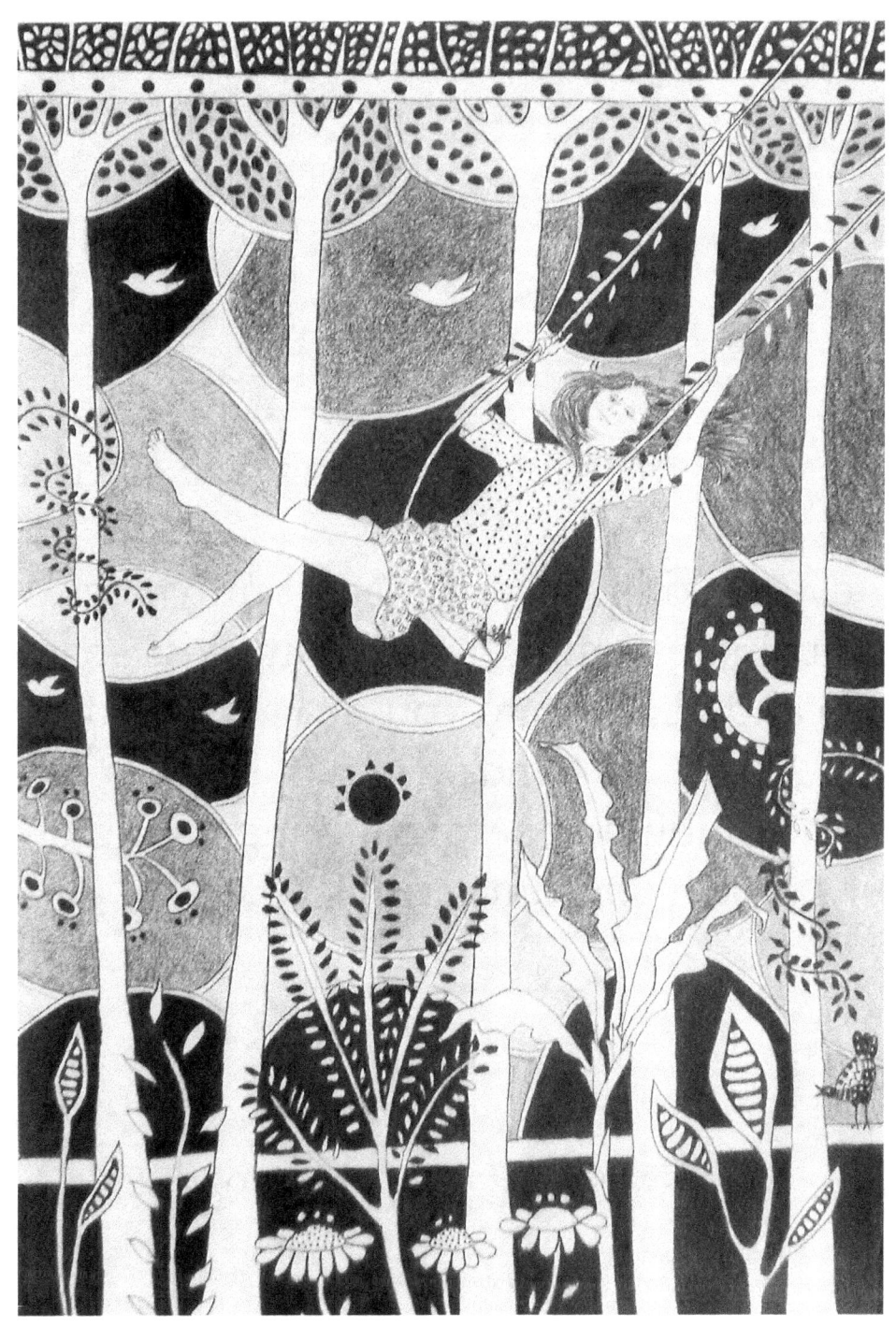

Swing

"I am she of the skies, wheeling free on dream
soft wings,
eyes gazing toward distant universes.
my being reaching beyond limitless space,
I am and I beckon to you dear heart, to join
and share
our combined energies giving us flight,
beyond time and infinity."

From" Who Am I", ©1988

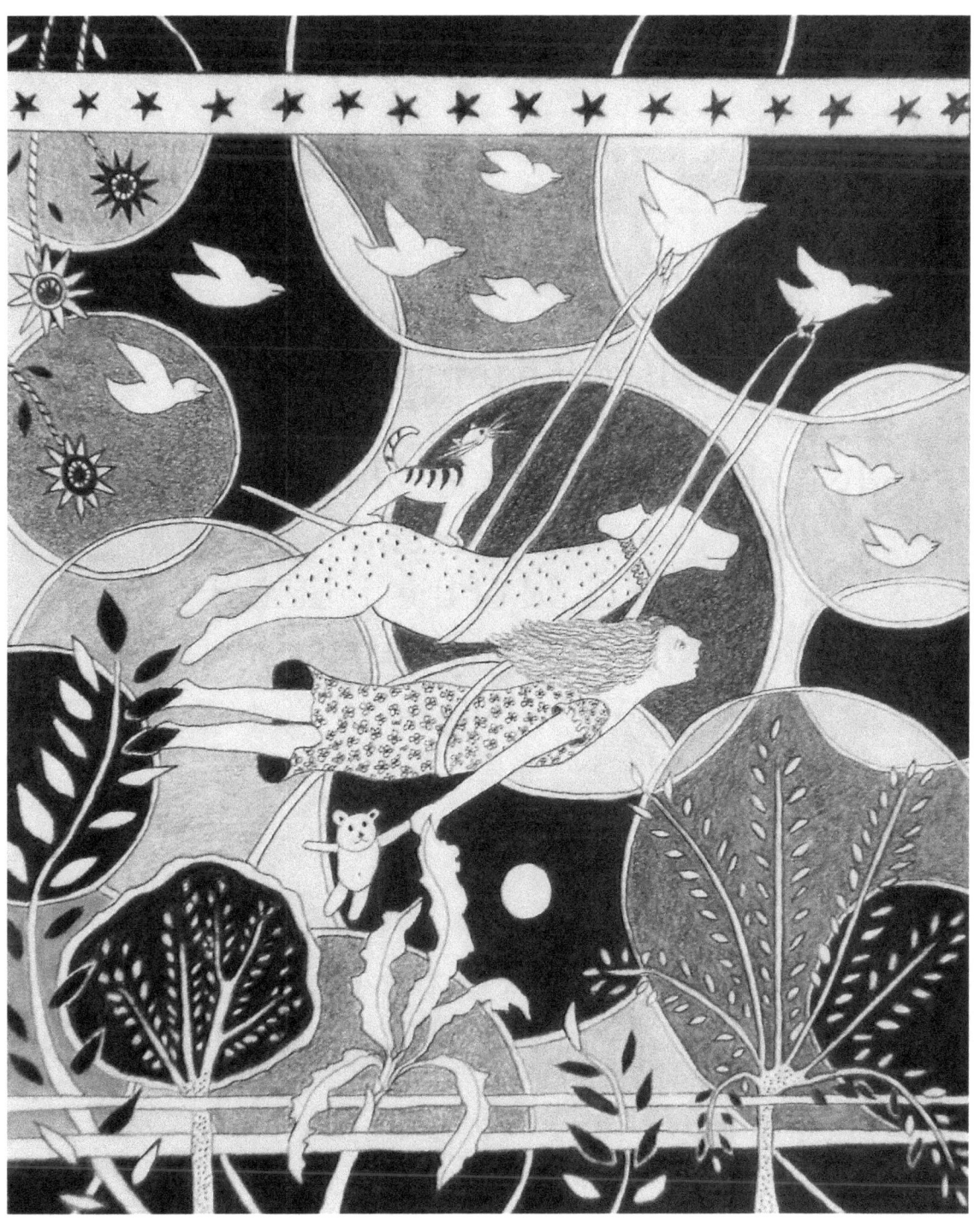

Dreams

"Her energies, gathered from the
stuff of the universe, are
Limitless.
Her body no longer burdened with fleshed heaviness,
is transparent.
She is a child of the light and
dances among the stars,
with abandon."

From "Starchild of the Universe"
©1999

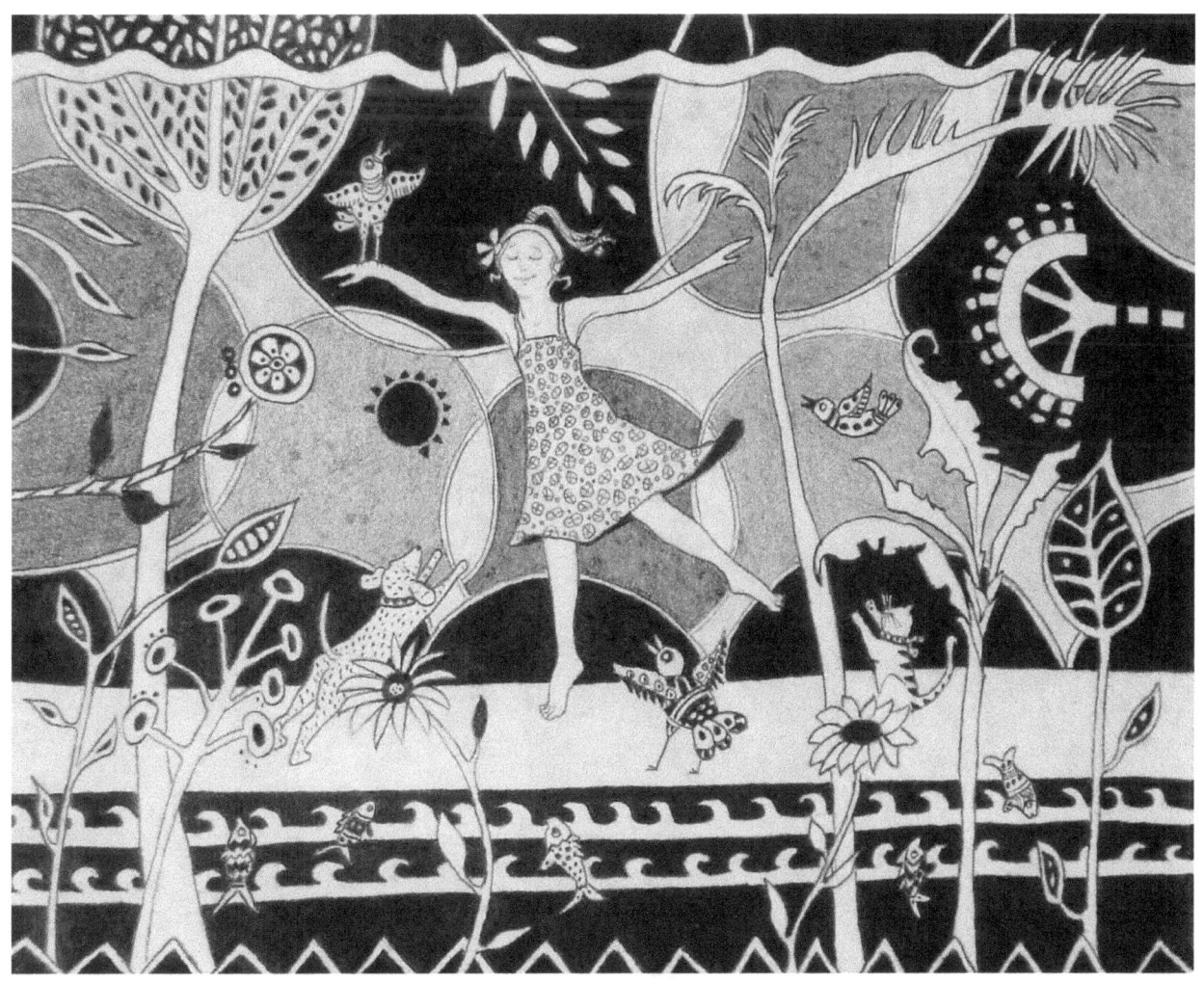

Dance

Cassandra was born in New Orleans, raised in South America and educated in Europe. Her work spans a 30-year career as a professional artist. Her work has been shown in galleries and museums across the USA and in Europe, received numerous awards and is part of many corporate and private collections. She has published 5 books and participated in two group publications. She is a member of the National Association of Women Artists in New York and is listed in "Who's Who of American Women", as curator and educator. She currently lives and works in her studio in New Mexico.

Sandra J Melcher, 1932-2020, American artist, poet. Born in Lockwood, OH, Sandra spent most of her married life in Florida. She was a Board Member Arts Council of Manatee County, Bradenton, 1996-1998; Member Florida Artist Group; Founder & President Digital Artist Group 1998-2003, Bradenton, Fl.; Member of Bradenton Yacht Club, Mentor Harbor Yacht Club (president Wet Hens 1979-1985), Chagrin Lagoons Yacht Club (pres. Gallery Maids 1977).